THE AMERICAN
CIVIL WAR IN TEXAS

Johanna Burke

NEW YORK

Published in 2010 by The Rosen Publishing Group, Inc.
29 East 21st Street, New York, NY 10010

Book Design: Michael J. Flynn

Photo Credits: Cover (soldiers firing cannon), cover (Texas flag), cover, pp. 3, 4, 6, 10, 14, 20, 22, 28,
30, 31, 32 (Texas emblem on all), 3–32 (textured background), 12 (stamp), 16 (statue), 17 (badge),
20–21 (landscape), back cover (Texas flag) © Shutterstock.com; pp. 5 (map), 20 (map) © GeoAtlas;
pp. 6–7 (battle scene), 28 (Lincoln and African Americans) © MPI/Hulton Archive/Getty Images;
pp. 7 (Sam Houston), 14 (Jefferson Davis) © Stock Montage/Hulton Archive/Getty Images;
p. 9 (Abraham Lincoln) © Katherine Young/Hulton Archive/Getty Images; pp. 11 (petition),
27 (Brownsville scene) © Texas State Library and Archives Commission; pp. 14 (Benjamin McCulloch),
15 (Rangers), 19 (Lawrence Sullivan Ross), 21 (Henry Hopkins Sibley) Wikimedia Commons;
pp. 18 (Sterling Price), 23 (ship) © Hulton Archive/Getty Images; p. 22 (General John Magruder) ©
Kean Collection/Hulton Archive/Getty Images; p. 24 (General William Franklin) © Time & Life Pictures/
Getty Images.

Library of Congress Cataloging-in-Publication Data

Burke, Johanna.
  The American Civil War in Texas / Johanna Burke.
      p. cm. — (Spotlight on Texas)
  Includes bibliographical references and index.
  ISBN 978-1-61532-472-9 (pbk.)
  ISBN 978-1-61532-473-6 (6-pack)
  ISBN 978-1-61532-474-3 (library binding)
  1. Texas—History—Civil War, 1861-1865—Juvenile literature. I. Title.
  E532.B87 2010
  976.4'05—dc22
                                    2009031318

Manufactured in the United States of America

CPSIA Compliance Information: Batch # WW1ORC: For further information contact Rosen Publishing, New York, New York at 1-800-237-9932.

CONTENTS

A DIVIDED NATION

The United States was still a young country in the mid-1800s, but it was quickly growing in size and power. Several problems had also been growing since the late 1700s. Some states wanted strong state governments. Others wanted a strong national government. The North and South disagreed about slavery. In the North, money was made through manufacturing. The South, on the other hand, made money from large farms called plantations, which used slaves. These differences led to the American Civil War (1861–1865). During this war, the Northern states became known as the Union. The Southern states were called the **Confederacy**.

Texans had fought for many years to become part of the United States. However, they sided with the Southern states on several important matters. In this book, you'll learn about the American Civil War and its effect on Texas.

A civil war is a war between two different groups of people within a country. This map shows what the United States looked like during the American Civil War and which side each state was on.

THE UNITED STATES IN 1861

- UNION STATES
- CONFEDERATE STATES
- SLAVE STATES IN UNION
- U.S. TERRITORIES

A Nation and a State

Texas was once part of Mexico. At the time, most Texans were originally from the United States. They didn't like the way the Mexican government treated them. They wanted to keep their old ways of life, but the Mexican government wanted them to follow Mexican laws and ways of life. In 1835, they began the Texas **Revolution** to gain their independence.

In 1836, the **Republic** of Texas became an independent country. War hero Samuel Houston became its first president. Texans worked hard to create a strong nation.

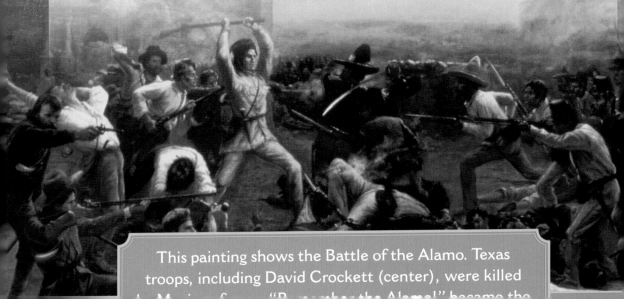

This painting shows the Battle of the Alamo. Texas troops, including David Crockett (center), were killed

Samuel Houston: Texas Hero

Samuel Houston joined the U.S. Army when he was 20 and quickly rose through the ranks. He became a Tennessee congressman in 1823. In 1827, he became governor of Tennessee. Later he moved to Texas, where he joined the Texas fight for freedom. He led troops during the Texas Revolution and soon became a major general in the Texas army. Houston served two terms as president of the Republic of Texas. He also served as governor of Texas after it became a U.S. state.

Houston was a proud Texan, but he also valued his U.S. citizenship. When problems arose between the Northern and Southern states, Houston believed Texas should side with the Northern states. Many other Texans disagreed with him.

Samuel Houston

Texas was a republic from 1836 to 1845. It had several problems during that time. Texas leaders often disagreed about how to run the country. Some leaders wanted to claim land west of Texas and move Native Americans out of the area. Others wanted to make peace with the Native Americans. Also, Texas was a small nation that had trouble guarding itself from Mexico. Some Texans believed that joining the United States would help them become safer and more powerful.

The U.S. Congress voted to make Texas a state in 1845. As the United States came closer to civil war, many Texans began siding with Southern states. Many Texas families owned slaves. Most Texans thought slavery was necessary for the success of their state.

Abraham Lincoln was against the spread of slavery in the United States. He was elected president in 1860. Many Texans thought Lincoln's election was a danger to their way of life. They decided to side with the other Southern states.

Abraham Lincoln

TEXAS JOINS THE CONFEDERACY

In December 1860, South Carolina became the first state to **secede**, or withdraw, from the United States. Other Southern states met to talk about seceding. Many Texas leaders and citizens wanted to discuss secession. However, Governor Houston believed Texas should remain in the United States. He called a special meeting of the Texas government. He warned them that seceding would weaken the South, allowing the North to win a civil war.

Against Houston's wishes, state officials met in Austin on January 28, 1861. They voted 166 to 8 in favor of seceding. A public vote was held on February 23. More than 46,000 Texans voted to secede, and only about 14,500 voted to stay in the United States. The large majority of Texans wanted to join the Confederacy.

Shown here is the first page of a letter signed by Texans and given to Sam Houston in 1860. The people who signed the letter urged Houston to discuss secession with Texas lawmakers.

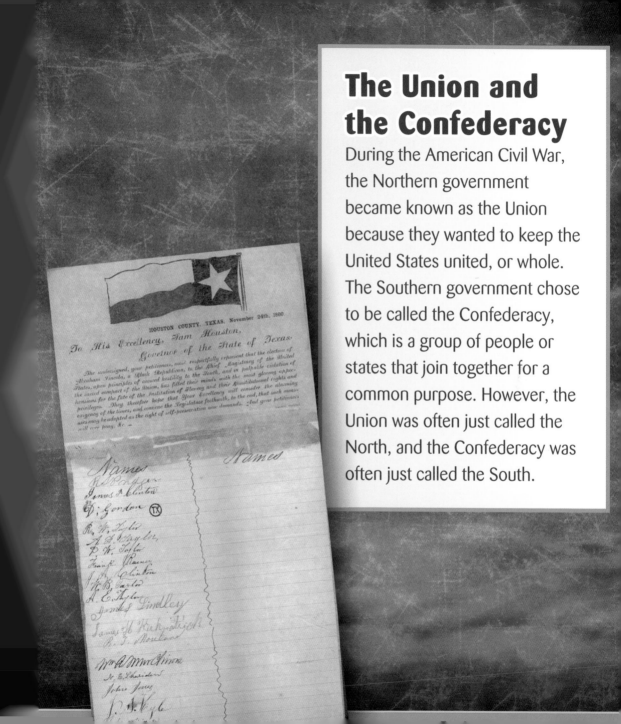

The Union and the Confederacy

During the American Civil War, the Northern government became known as the Union because they wanted to keep the United States united, or whole. The Southern government chose to be called the Confederacy, which is a group of people or states that join together for a common purpose. However, the Union was often just called the North, and the Confederacy was often just called the South.

On March 5, 1861, Texas leaders met again to announce that Texas was seceding from the United States. Governor Houston once again tried to keep Texas from joining the Confederacy.

Leaders voted for Texas to become a member of the Confederate States of America. Houston would not promise to obey the Confederacy and was removed from office by the new Confederate government of Texas. President Abraham Lincoln offered to send U.S. troops to help keep Texas in the Union. Houston turned down the offer to avoid bloodshed in Texas.

Upon being removed from office, Samuel Houston moved to Huntsville, Texas. He died there on July 26, 1863. Shown here is a 1964 stamp honoring Houston.

Houston's **lieutenant governor**, Edward Clark, became the first governor of Texas under the Confederacy. In an August 1861 election, Francis R. Lubbock beat Clark to become the second governor.

Clark and Lubbock

Neither Clark nor Lubbock were originally from Texas. Clark was born in New Orleans, Louisiana, in 1815. He spent the first part of his life in Georgia and Alabama. In 1841, Clark moved to Texas and opened a law office. He became a respected officer and government official.

Lubbock was born in Beaufort, South Carolina, in 1815. He moved first to Louisiana, and then to Texas in 1836. He opened a general store and had a ranch. Soon he became involved in Texas politics.

The election of 1861 was very close. Lubbock won by 124 votes! Both men soon became Confederate officers. After the war, Clark and Lubbock both returned to their jobs and families in Texas.

THE CALL TO ARMS

The Confederate government—led by President Jefferson Davis—put Colonel Benjamin McCulloch in charge of the Texas army. McCulloch was a Texas Ranger who had fought for the United States in the war against Mexico. On February 16, 1861, McCulloch and about 500 **volunteers** surrounded the Union troops at the Alamo in San Antonio. The general in charge at the Alamo **surrendered** all Union property in Texas to the Confederacy. Soon after, about 2,700 Union soldiers peacefully left Texas.

Benjamin McCulloch

Jefferson Davis

Texas Rangers

The Texas Rangers were originally hired to "range" or travel around Texas and guard settlers from Native American attacks. During the Texas Revolution, they served as scouts, spies, soldiers, and guides. During the Mexican-American War, the Rangers became famous for their bravery in battle. Stories about the Rangers became popular all over the country. Most people didn't know that the Rangers sometimes used unnecessary force to solve problems.

Since the Civil War, the Texas Rangers have fulfilled many other duties for the state of Texas. Today, the Rangers are a special branch of the Texas state police force. Many people still think of the brave fighters of the Wild West when talking about the Texas Rangers.

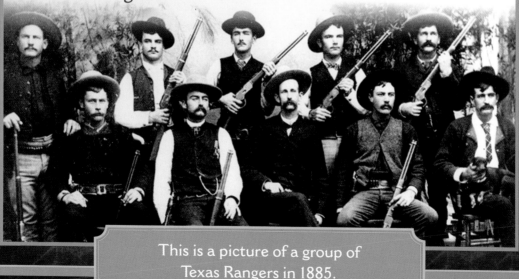

This is a picture of a group of Texas Rangers in 1885.

The Texas government continued to sign up soldiers. Texas's main job during the American Civil War was to send soldiers and supplies to guard the state in the southwest and along the Gulf of Mexico.

In total, the Confederacy signed about 90,000 Texan soldiers during the American Civil War. About two-thirds of the soldiers were in the cavalry—the men who fought on horseback. This was because most Texans were excellent riders.

In 1861, Confederate leaders requested that Texas send troops to fight in Virginia. As many as 25,000 Texas soldiers had joined the Confederate army by late 1861. Confederate leaders valued Texas soldiers because they were experienced and brave in battle. Many had fought in the Mexican-American War and the Texas Revolution. Confederate leaders often sent small groups of Texas Rangers ahead of the main force to carry out surprise attacks on the enemy. They were also used to raid enemy supplies and block their messages.

Texas Ranger badge

Texans fought in every major Civil War battle. However, most Texas soldiers remained in Texas. Many helped guard Texas borders against attacks from Northern troops, Native Americans, and Mexicans. Most battles occurred along the eastern coast. Texas struggled to guard the western border, too, which became known as the "back door" of the Confederacy.

Other Texans were ordered to capture western territories far away from the main battles of the American Civil War. Texas became a base for Confederate troops in the west. Several troops crossed the northern border and easily captured Northern forts in Indian Territory (today Oklahoma). Others were sent to gain control of New Mexico and Arizona.

Sterling Price

Major General Sterling Price fought battles for the Confederacy north of Texas, mainly in Arkansas and Missouri.

Lawrence Sullivan Ross

Lawrence Sullivan Ross was a Texas Ranger and Confederate general. He became the nineteenth Texas governor in 1887.

THE NEW MEXICO CAMPAIGN

In 1862, Texas troops led by General Henry Hopkins Sibley tried to capture the land between Texas and the Pacific coast. The Confederacy hoped to gain control of gold mines in Colorado and ports in California. This became known as the New Mexico campaign because part of it took place in New Mexico Territory.

Sibley's troops won several battles, but the campaign was largely unsuccessful. Sibley's troops failed to take important forts along the way, and about one-third of the soldiers died. Sibley returned to Texas. The North sent more troops to protect their land in the southwest. They even occupied some forts in western Texas. By this time, there were not enough Confederate troops to retake the southwest.

The red line on this modern map shows the route taken

Henry Hopkins Sibley

Henry Hopkins Sibley had been an officer during the Mexican-American War. After the war, he became very familiar with the western **frontier** while stationed in Texas, Kansas, Utah, and New Mexico. Sibley went to see Confederate president Jefferson Davis to suggest the New Mexico campaign. He became a general and led the Texas troops during the campaign. Many believe it was Sibley's fault that the campaign failed.

Henry Hopkins Sibley

BATTLES IN TEXAS

Union attacks in and around Texas were planned to interrupt the flow of supplies to eastern forces. Texas troops were able to defend the coast, but the Northern navy set up a **blockade** to keep Confederate supply ships from entering and leaving gulf ports. The main attack against the Texas coast began late in 1862. Eight Northern ships attacked the largest Texas port in Galveston and easily took control.

On January 1, 1863, the Confederate army—led by General John Magruder—staged a surprise attack on Northern forces in Galveston. Magruder's forces retook the city of Galveston, sunk a Northern ship, and chased the others away from the port. This event became known as the Battle of Galveston. Texas held Galveston for the rest of the war.

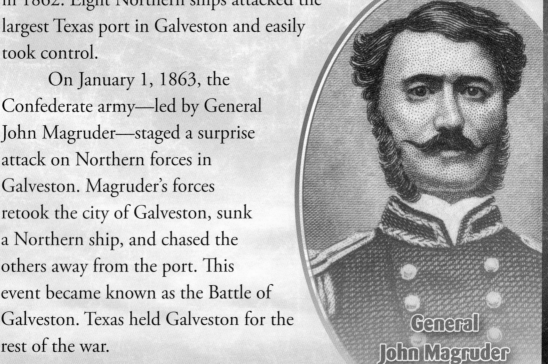

General John Magruder

Confederate ships
Union ships

Pelican Spit

stuck in sand

sunken

sunken

Galveston

GULF OF MEXICO

The Confederates only had two ships, and one was sunk early in the battle. The other sunk a Union ship and chased the rest away.

The Confederate navy used ships called "runners" to break through the Northern blockade in the Gulf of Mexico. The *Lizzie*, shown here, was captured while carrying supplies to Galveston from Cuba.

The North continued to attack the Texas coast, hoping to break Confederate supply lines. In September 1863, General William Franklin led 4,000 Northern soldiers from New Orleans to the mouth of the Sabine River. This river forms part of the border between Texas and Louisiana. Franklin planned to sail eleven ships into the river and beat Confederate troops at Fort Griffin. He then planned to land his ships in Sabine Lake, where the troops would begin their march to Houston.

General
William Franklin

The Confederate soldiers in Fort Griffin captured 300 Northern soldiers and two gunboats. The Confederate government gave Dowling and the forty-seven men under his command medals for their bravery.

However, Franklin had misjudged the power of the Confederate troops led by Lieutenant Richard W. Dowling. When Franklin's ships got close, the Confederate troops fired cannons at them. They sank several Union ships. The rest quickly turned back. Texas Confederates had won the Battle of Sabine Pass.

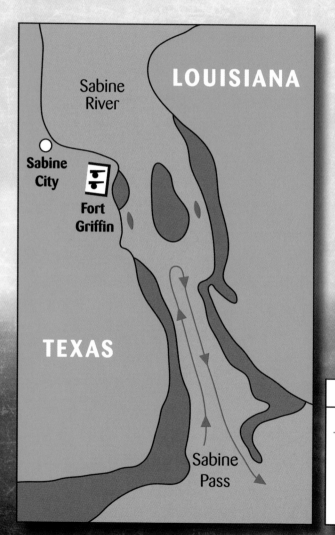

LOUISIANA

Sabine River

Sabine City

Fort Griffin

TEXAS

Sabine Pass

Key

→ path of Union ships

sunken Union ships

Confederate cannons

In late 1863, Northern troops gained control of the Texas coast from Brownsville to Corpus Christi. This cut off shipping trade between Texas and Mexico. However, Confederate troops soon took back much of the coast.

The Confederacy had begun to weaken, thanks in part to a lack of supplies. In April 1865, Confederate commander Robert E. Lee surrendered, ending the American Civil War. However, some troops for both sides in Texas continued to fight. Even today, the reasons for this are not clear.

The last battle of the war occurred at Palmito Ranch near the city of Brownsville on May 12, 1865. Northern troops attacked Confederates there who had refused to give up. Both sides were tired, but extra soldiers led by Major John "Rip" Ford arrived and helped the Confederates win the Battle of Palmito Ranch.

Even though Texas Confederates won the final battle, Union soldiers later forced the Confederate troops out of Brownsville.

John "Rip" Ford

Rip Ford was one of Texas's more colorful officers. By the time the American Civil War started, Ford was a skilled soldier and Texas Ranger. He had also been a doctor and a newspaper editor. Ford had served in the Texas state legislature before the war. In 1874, Ford became mayor of Brownsville, and in 1876 he served in the Texas senate again.

Confederate forces leaving Brownsville

TEXAS AFTER THE WAR

On June 19, 1865, Northern troops led by General Gordon Granger arrived in Galveston. Granger read a special paper written by President Abraham Lincoln stating that all slaves were now free.

After the war, fighting continued between Texans who wanted to secede and those who voted to stay in the United States. Texas farmers had a hard time learning to make a living without slavery. Northern troops remained in Texas for years to enforce laws against slavery. Texas was not welcomed back into the United States until 1870. Life in Texas remained hard for many years. In time, however, Texas recovered from the Civil War. Thanks to new practices such as cattle herding and oil drilling, Texas soon became an important and powerful state.

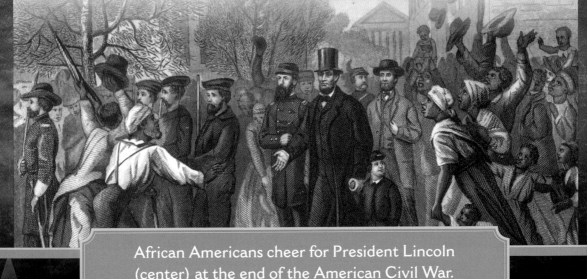

African Americans cheer for President Lincoln (center) at the end of the American Civil War.

TIMELINE OF THE AMERICAN CIVIL WAR IN TEXAS

December 29, 1845 — Texas becomes the twenty-eighth state in the United States.

November 6, 1860 — Abraham Lincoln is elected president of the United States.

December 20, 1860 — South Carolina becomes the first state to secede from the Union.

January 28, 1861 — Texas leaders vote in favor of seceding from the Union.

February 16, 1861 — Texas forces take control of the Alamo; Northern forces begin leaving the state.

February 23, 1861 — Citizens of Texas vote to secede.

March 5, 1861 — Texas officials announce the state is seceding.

February 1862 — General Henry Hopkins Sibley begins the New Mexico campaign.

January 1, 1863 — Battle of Galveston

September 8, 1863 — Battle of Sabine Pass

April 1865 — The Confederacy surrenders, ending the American Civil War.

May 12, 1865 — Battle of Palmito Ranch

June 19, 1865 — Union troops led by General Gordon Granger arrive in Galveston.

March 30, 1870 — Texas is allowed back into the United States.

READER RESPONSE PROJECTS

- Choose one of the military leaders discussed in this book. Use the Internet and library sources to learn more about the person you chose. Write a short biography of the person and tell about the events in his life leading up to the American Civil War. You may also include facts about the person's life after the war.

- Imagine that you were at the meeting where Texas leaders voted to secede in 1860. Would you have voted for or against secession? Write a letter explaining why you voted the way you did, and try to convince other Texans to agree with your opinions.

- Imagine that you are a Texas Ranger during the American Civil War. Draw a picture of a battle. Include details you read about in this book.

GLOSSARY

blockade (blah-KAYD) A group of ships that stops other ships from entering or leaving a port.

Confederacy (kuhn-FEH-duh-ruh-see) The name for the Southern states during the American Civil War.

frontier (frun-TIHR) The edge of a settled country, where the wilderness begins.

lieutenant governor (loo-TEH-nuhnt GUH-vuhn-uhr) A person who is second in control behind the governor.

republic (rih-PUH-blihk) A form of government in which the people elect the leaders who run the government.

revolution (reh-vuh-LOO-shun) A war against the government in power.

secede (sih-SEED) To withdraw from a group or country.

surrender (suh-REHN-duhr) To give up.

volunteer (vah-luhn-TIHR) Someone who gives their time without pay.

INDEX

Due to the changing nature of Internet links, the Rosen Publishing Group, Inc., has developed an online list of Web sites related to the subject of this book. This site is updated regularly. Please use this link to access the list: **http://www.rcbmlinks.com/sot/civtex/**